# PASSENGERS OF LIFE

## Daniele Kieraite

BookLeaf Publishing

India | USA | UK

Presentation by *BookLeaf Publishing*

Web: www.bookleafpub.com

E-mail: info@bookleafpub.com

ISBN: 9789358361117

First edition 2021

For those who dream big and stay
strong despite the storm.

# PREFACE

Plenty of people cross our paths, but how many of them touch our hearts? All of us create various relationships throughout our lifetimes, starting from family members, then moving to friends, maybe romantic partners or people who we can only admire from afar. Other connections include co-workers or like-minded peers with who we share our passions or hobbies.

Sadly, not all of those bonds work out for various reasons, such as sudden death, rough argument, gradual separation, or some people simply vanish and leave us with many unanswered questions. However, sometimes we are the ones who leave someone behind.

No matter how far we come, how much we achieve or how many other new people we come across, some connections will always stay in our hearts and remind us of moments when we laughed, cried, discovered something new, felt grateful, inspired or lost hope and a part of ourselves that only a specific person was able to bring.

Passengers of life is a poetry book that comes from a young heart that already experienced both joy and pain and still tries to make sense of some things that happened. This book is also a tribute to the people we lose forever and only realise their worth after their death. In my case, I unexpectedly lost my cousin in June 2019.

Some of you might be able to relate to my personal experiences on an emotional level and maybe even recognise your own feelings. I wrote this book aiming to inspire and remind you that some things that occur do not define you as a person, and even if sometimes it looks like life will always stay horrible, it won't, and the sun will shine again. Maybe initially, it will hesitate to shine, but the golden sunrise will light up the sky one day again.

# 1. Passengers of Life

Seasons change and the people go,

Leaving past behind

Life will continue its flow,

Despite the feelings passing by.


One day you share a smile with the ones you love,

On another, you might shed a tear

When tomorrow is unknown,

The present is a gift.


Passengers of life are changing fast,

Some of them just leave

Others have to die,

Only the special people will stay inside.

Enjoy this day and share your feelings,

As this chance might be the last

But do not regret the things that happened,

As the change won't pass.

# 2. Mum

You were always there for me,

When I was all alone and crying

You brushed my tears and cast away my fears,

You, my mum, are always here beside me.


You have always put me first,

And have never broken my trust

You showed me the love,

When I left myself abandoned.


Sometimes I become afraid,

Of thoughts that one day you will leave me

All alone in this dynamic world,

As you are everything, I have.

I am grateful for your sacrifices,

And endless patience

You are someone I will never forget,

As you are the reason why I am alive.

# 3. Sacred Soul

He was living here with us,

Carrying the silent wisdom in his youth

He loved to read and to dream big,

When he was all alone at home.


Sometimes crowds surrounded him,

And saw him as a party lion or a fool

But his mother known another truth,

That he felt misread within.


He was always kind to family,

By putting them before himself

And always offered genuine assistance,

That was liked but not the way he lived.


He never had a pile of money,

Or an influential status

As not these things would make him happy,

When his soul craved for a vivid journey.


Only after sudden death,

He became a hero for the family

As his funeral was big and brought regretful tears,

That felt like a late apology.


For me, he was more than just a cousin,

As he held my hand when my mother couldn't

He used to guide me to the kindergarten,

And always listened to what I spoke.


He was never someone who would judge,

Or someone who would hold a grudge

He always knew when he should smile,

Even when the pain was kept in silence.

There are a lot of things I never told,

Even that I'm thankful for his roles

Of a father and a brother who I lost,

And never had a chance to hold him close.

## 4.  Father

You were never there for me, your child,

When I was taking my first steps

Even at my best, you've been absent,

As you cared more about yourself.


When I walked to my first class,

Other kids had both their parents

I did not show it to my mum,

How in the crowd I looked for you.


In my teenage years, I felt alone and
worried,

And my mental health was slowly
dropping

I had no friends around that time,

As from the crowd, I was excluded.

Even when the depression came around,

And all I wanted was to die

Still, you have never called or asked,

How your daughter's life is going?


When I moved to another country,

And began the university

Still, you have never called or asked,

How your daughter's life is going?


All I ever wanted as a child,

Was to have you by my side

But you never felt the same,

And left me like I was never here.


Even though you left me scars,

I learned to heal them on my own

Sometimes wounds hurt like they are fresh,

Still, I try to ease the pain how I can do my best.


All I know about you,

Is that you hurt those around you

You often walk alone, just like a wolf,

And like to blame the others for your faults.


For a while, I tried to blame myself and understand,

Why I was never loved by my father

Maybe everything was meant to be this way,

That you had to walk away.


Books and life experience have taught me,

That you have to love yourself

To pour that feeling into others,

So I wish you all the best in learning
how to love yourself.

# 5.  Grandma

You helped my mum to raise me,

Had been beside me since my first words

You always listened to my stories,

And let me know how much you care.


I grew up in your small town,

Surrounded by nature's calmness

As a kid, I didn't know the value,

Of serenity and peace of life.


In summer, I observed the sky, birds and flowers,

Climbed on our trees or sometimes through the window

I liked to do it, even though you didn't,

As it made me feel bold and stronger.

You also taught me how to pray,

As you believe in God's power

You have never doubted in your faith,

Even when the love of your life was
taken away.


You, not mum, showed me how to cook,

When the sickness came to you

You also deeply love the plants,

So you told me how to nurture them.


I am thankful for your presence,

And an endless amount of love

You are more than Grandma,

You are my second mum.

# 6. Relative

I saw you as a little baby,

Peacefully sleeping in your mother's arms

When your parents introduced us,

At our Grandma's house.


The years have passed, and we have grown,

Eventually, became more close

By playing with stuffed animals and dolls,

And sharing our thoughts.


I saw you as a little sister that I've never had,

Who I hoped to keep in my long-term life

Until you became like Brutus,

Who stabbed Caesar's back.

# 7. Cousin/Brother

We used to have some conversations

About the music, life and fashion,

You have acted as my mentor

And became my first male authority.


Sometimes I saw you as emotionless and cold

As often you didn't like to open up,

Maybe I also didn't really show

How much I loved our time.


You introduced me to Electronic music

And advised me how to change my style,

Sometimes you enjoyed roasting me

And discussed with me about your plans.

There's a picture of when you held me as a baby

And you seemed to be genuinely happy,

Even though we now don't see each other

You will always be like my real brother.

# 8. Godparents

Both of you gave me many gifts,

During my early development days

You helped my mother and Grandma to raise me,

And treated me as your own little girl.


Together we spent so many summers,

By talking under our old Chestnut tree

Back then, it felt like a routine,

But now it's just a beautiful memory.


I enjoyed playing with your Dachshunds,

And together marking annual celebrations

I loved greeting the both of you with a hug,

And felt sad when saying Goodbye.

I never said out loud how much I care,

But I do, and I feel really thankful

For your presence and genuine help,

You, my Godparents, will always be special people in my life.

# 9. Family Leader

When I was little, you often showed how much you loved me,

You used to hug me and let me know that you have missed me

Sometimes you would bring me gifts or tell sweet words,

Until I closed my childhood's doors

When I changed my nature in my teenage years,

Sometimes your words have left some tears

You liked to show who is the boss,

Which has later turned into a painful loss

You even tried to stop me from achieving my dream,

When you picked an emotional manipulation

When I was deciding between staying and leaving,

A lack of support guided me into the real meaning

Of understanding who actually cares,

And who wasn't there in the first place

I used to view you as an authority,

Until your presence stopped making me happy

Eventually, I closed off myself emotionally,

As you criticised everything that I liked, honestly

Sometimes I wonder: "Where your love has gone?"

"Was it when I made decisions on my own?"

"Or when I moved far away from you?"

I guess only you can know the answers,

As you're the one who brought the tensions.

# 10.  Grandparents

I remember your shiny eyes and a big smile

When you visited me after a while,

You always showed a genuine interest

In my life's events and inner feelings.


You are always very proud of me

Despite the moments when I fail,

You are one of a few

Who told me that I could trust my heart and follow the unknown.


Grandma, I will always be deeply grateful

For your emotional support and kindness,

During my personally turbulent phases

When I had no one left to call.


You and Grandpa showed me how to give

Unconditionally for those that you love,

As you have never asked for anything in return

So thank you for all of your efforts and support.

# 11. Childhood Friend

Both of us loved a fantasy world

When we met in a primary school

We liked to create and imagine

Things that only lived in our heads.


We had pets dinosaurs and animal spirits

That would follow our steps

Sometimes we identified as princesses

Who know the magical secrets.


You were my very first friend

And a wonderful click

For childish mental stimulation

And a budding mind of creation.

Even though you suddenly broke my trust

When I introduced you to another friend

Till that final moment, I will always recall

Our special friendship out of this world.

# 12. Long-distance Friend

You looked shy at your family's gathering,

When we saw each other for the first time

Then I had to pluck up my courage,

And be the first who says: "Hi."


Back then, we had many mutual interests,

Just like the music, similar perspectives

We wanted to see each other more often,

But we lived from each other too far.


You always seemed so happy to see me,

As you would show how much you missed me

Once you invited me to visit your family near the sea,

And really took care of all of my needs.


Sadly, now we don't talk so often,

As we are located even further

One of the things that I want you to know,

Is that I always valued you, even when I didn't show.

# 13. Blond Girl

You knew what to say just to make me laugh in tears,

From the moment I saw you, I knew we would be friends

Your beauty was something I was craving to have,

Like the adventures, you have made with other pals

Now that you're gone, only pictures remind me of you,

I hope that you know I will always send positive vibes to you

Despite you might think that it is only my fault,

Because I was the one who ended our bond.

## 14.  Fellow Creative

We enjoyed the deep conversations

About the art of life and situations,

Both of us had been creative

And kinda felt alienated.


We've met online almost accidentally

Through a shared passion for artistry,

You used to be my inspiration

As you had a huge motivation.


We would chat for many hours

And share some bright ideas,

That never came to fruition

As they stayed in the planning stages.


One thing that I can't understand

Is why you suddenly left,

I always wished you all the best

And hoped to see you shining like a star.

# 15.  Self-Confident Friend

We became friends when we felt alone,

Your best friend has left you in the cold

Most of the classmates closed their
doors to you,

And I decided to make a room in my life
for you.


I did that cause I knew,

What it's like to be excluded

When life's circumstances do not
depend on you,

And all that's left is hope that better
things are coming through.


Our friendship had a strong dynamic,

Of joyful laugh and painful tears

We've made some memories,

Those were meant to fade away.

You showed me how to look to be
attractive,

How to have that sense of confidence

You also brought the pain along the way,

When your words cut my soul in a way.


You are the first person who I planned a
birthday gift,

The one I gathered through six months

I really wanted your appreciation,

As you had my friendly admiration.


Once we partied with classmates,

Then you said: "I love you" phrase

It brought me unexpected tears,

As for the first time, I felt loved by my
friend...

# 16. The Lost Friend

Yesterday you left me full of questions,

When you  abandoned me like others

You are different than they all,

As you left me zero clues.


I was always there beside you,

When the pain had only drowned you

You liked to talk but not to listen,

My energy might be too much giving.


You broke me twice and then came back,

I believed you missed our friendship after the separation

You looked excited to reunite,

Even said that we were never meant to fall apart.

You are the first who I cooked the food,

The first who agreed on life's views

You also played me like a doll,

When you practised push and pull.


On some nights, you've shared your
poetry with me,

That talked about your want to end your
life

As I was naïve and fearful,

I kept it as our friendship's secret.


One evening we drunk girly,

And the red wine spilt the ceiling

I thought that night would bring good
vibes,

But it was meant to make me
traumatised.

In the middle of a dark night,

You attempted to cut your veins with a
cutlery knife

I pleaded you to stop and tried to hide a
tragic gun,

But the damage was already done.


After a vicious night, our bond was still
remaining,

When on winter you've attempted
suicide

Even then, I came to see your face,

Hoping that this time your life will be
alright.


We continued talking for a year,

And you tied a red bracelet on my wrist

That was your travel gift,

Before I left my native place.

Then you were still a part of my life,

Shared your thoughts and gave advice

Somehow we began to have less talk,

Until the argument has struck.


I thought that you deleted me
completely,

Until one day your message reached me

Sadly, our connection did not last for
long,

I feel that now you left me for good.


This time you left no explanation and
only wonder,

If I was ever doing something good

Probably we won't speak again, but I
want you to know,

That I will always wish you happiness
and peace.

# 17. Mysterious Boy

One of the things that hurt me the most,

Is that I dedicated you so many songs

To me, they are so beautiful and special,

Like I thought that you are.


I was ready to give you all of what I
have,

All of my love, care and affection

Just to have you longer in my life,

But nothing of that mattered to you.


I was trying to win your love,

By changing myself and smiling at you

But feelings for you dimmed my light
and passion for life

Because you wanted a calm girl waiting
for you.

It took me some time to realise,

That I will never be her, as my inner fire
is too strong

I can't be someone else,

For a boy, I will never have.


I wasted so many days,

Hoping to hear those special words

Probably it was my biggest mistake,

Because you never felt the same.


Today I am releasing you from my mind
and a heart,

Because I welcome the new

Goodbye, beautiful boy,

A mystery that I will never solve...

# 18. Intellectual Friend

Sometimes I find myself questioning

Whether our friendship is genuine,

We might hurt each other with words

Often when our hearts are closed.


I really wanted to see you last time

And share all of what was on my mind,

But I didn't, because I had a fear

That you won't like what you will hear.


We both feel that we can't open to each other

You, as you know that your words can cut me,

Me, cause I feel that some things should be unsaid

Yet, we still call each other friends.

We agree on deeper values

And have some intellectual discussions,

All we have to do is trust the present

And allow life to guide our direction.

# 19. Sunshine

You seem to look always happy,

Around the ones you think of highly

Your smile can light everyone up,

Wherever you come to show up.


You met me at my lowest point,

When everything I knew was falling apart

Without any judgment, you let me in,

And supported me through thick and thin.


You showed me how it's like,

To know someone who has your back

With you, I slowly learn how to trust,

And how it feels to be loved by a friend.

Even though we've met quite recently,

You treat me like I belong to your family

I will always be grateful to you,

For being a beautiful Sunshine that lights up the sky.

# 20. I

There were moments,

When you saw yourself in a mirror

And couldn't stop the tears,

From falling down your face.


Back then, you felt small and lonely,

Instead of believing in your power

You almost forgot how to smile,

As there was no reason to feel alive.


When there was no one left to trust,

You began to fade yourself

For a few years, you sat in silence and pain,

Until the toxic environment was changed.

Deep inside, you craved for a positive change,

So you began to nurture yourself again

Slowly but surely, you started building yourself,

Until some people hurt you again.


Now you came back to yourself,

Trying to find what things do you want

On some days, you feel more sure of the direction,

While sometimes comes the sadness and pain resurrection.


Each day still looks like a lesson,

Which asks to deal with feelings

That sometimes can't be controlled,

As connections with others remain a mystery.

Even though your heart was really broken,

You still have lots of love for others

Some might think that the pain can make you heartless,

But it helped you recognise another hopeless.


When it feels like you are moving nowhere,

Remember the days when hope was regained

Life cannot be black or white,

As there would be no surprise.